Isle of Wight Railw

Compiled by Roger Simmonds

The
· Transport ·
Treasury

This book is dedicated to Frank Ash and all his colleagues

who took us all over the Island railway network.

© Images and design: The Transport Treasury 2020. Text Roger Simmonds.

ISBN 978-1-913251-12-3

First Published in 2020 by Transport Treasury Publishing Ltd. 16 Highworth Close, High Wycombe, HP13 7PJ

www.ttpublishing.co.uk

Printed in the UK by Henry Ling Limited, at the Dorset Press, Dorchester. DT1 1HD.

Contents

Front cover: No. 16 *Ventnor,* on a Cowes service, takes water at Newport in about 1963.

Title page: Appropriately, No. 16 *Ventnor* at Ventnor in the process of running round its train.

Opposite: A busy scene at the Pier Head around 1965. A Ventnor bound train occupies Platform One whilst a Cowes train awaits her turn in Platform Two. The 'O2' in Platform Four denotes the engine crew are on Roster number Five. This view shows the final layout at Ryde Pier Head following the considerable improvements carried out in the 1920s including the construction of Platform Four which instantly became Platform One as the SR reversed the numbering..!

Rear cover: The Newspaper proclaims a reprieve but it was a somewhat hollow victory as just Ryde to Shanklin was to survive the final cull of the once extensive network.

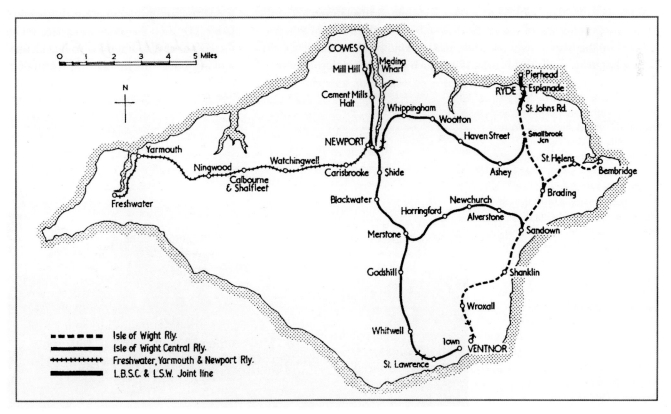

Introduction

The railways of the Isle of Wight have always had an enduring popularity with both visiting holiday makers and railway enthusiasts over many years from the day that Driver Alexander Hindmarsh opened the regulator and steamed out of Cowes in July 1862 with the very first train to run on the Island. From the preserve of the wealthy in the early days, shoot forward to the mid-20th century as holidays with pay expanded for the working classes, enabling visitors to make their way to the Island and become entranced by the "little trains" scurrying their way, criss-crossing the Island network, providing them with the experience of travelling in quaint elderly carriages to the holiday destination of choice. Growing numbers of enthusiasts were being drawn by the prospect of photographing 19th century locomotives and rolling stock, much of pre-grouping origin, well into the 1960s

From the early days of the 1860s and the emergence of photography, railways were a common subject to capture and the Island was no exception and many images thankfully survive. Several have been reproduced in various publications and for a comprehensive history of the Island railways the author highly recommends the series of Oakwood

Press Publications by Maycock & Silsbury. They have been a helpful reference point for this book.

I have focussed this book on the 1950s and 60s, the network still largely intact at the beginning of this period. Sadly the Merstone to Ventnor West line went first in 1952, unstaffing the stations and introducing push-pull working proving not enough to stem the financial losses. The following year saw the end for both Newport to Freshwater and Brading to Bembridge, the last trains running on 20 September. The former closure seriously isolated the West Wight despite some improvements to the bus service. Worse was to follow with the demise of Newport to Sandown in 1956 with the settlements in the middle of the Island no longer accessible by train, and would be passengers from Newport wishing to go to Ventnor now having to go via Ryde St Johns.

A decade of respite followed but the decision to go ahead and close the line from Smallbrook Junction via Newport to Cowes raised many eyebrows, Newport being the principal town and municipal centre. Maybe the growing pressure for road improvements around Newport was a compelling reason that opposition to BR closure plans

Driver Frankie Ash gives a cheery smile to the photographer at Ventnor circa 1963. He started his career at Newport shed as a cleaner around 1941, becoming a driver in 1959. Seen here in charge of No. 20 *Shanklin*, he recalled his favourite however was No. 18 *Ningwood*. He sadly died in 1979. *(Photo courtesy of Pete Ash.)*

Introduction

seemed rather muted from the Island authorities. Retaining Ryde to Ventnor had a compelling case – it made a profit! However, a working party decided in late 1964 to recommend curtailment of the line at Shanklin and set Ventnor adrift from the rail network. This was approved in July 1965. And so it was that the whole network shut down in December 1966 allowing the Ryde to Shanklin line to be electrified and adapted so ex-London tube stock could be used. Several reasons have been suggested for closing Shanklin to Ventnor, this including the saving of maintenance costs on the tunnel, and the resulting power drop on that section requiring an additional electricity generating substation at significant cost. Whatever the reason, the Ryde to Shanklin section re opened in March 1967 as an electrified line with a passing loop at Sandown and a double line from Ryde St Johns to Esplanade.

Probably unnoticed by most, but a former Isle of Wight Central Railway motif still in place in he 1960s as part of a station canopy support.

seems destined to repeat itself with further second-hand tube stock. At least in that way the last remnant of public railway will survive.

The images contained in this book are virtually all previously unpublished and are presented by a journey on each of the routes as they survived post-nationalisation. I have avoided much technical detail on matters such as rolling stock as this has been ably covered elsewhere in previous publications. Sadly post-war photographic coverage of the Ventnor West branch is limited but some recent images have come to light of Whitwell and Ventnor West.

As things stand in 2020 the existing tube stock is badly worn out, some parts are now non-existent and stock dwindles as spares are salvaged from donor vehicles. But there is hope even if history

There is a brief but wonderful snapshot video of St Lawrence and the terminus on YouTube: https://youtu.be/e4S3H_iu7wk

The author would like to thank Kevin Robertson for suggesting the idea for the book and his encouragement throughout, Pete Ash for allowing the use of the photograph of his father and providing information pertaining to his time on the Island railways.

Roger Simmonds. Ventnor 2020.

Bibliography

Isle of Wight Railways Remembered by Peter Paye, published by OPC.
The Isle of Wight Railway by Maycock & Silsbury, published by Oakwood Press.
The Isle of Wight Central Railway by Maycock & Silsbury, published by Oakwood Press.
The Freshwater, Yarmouth & Newport Railway by Maycock & Silsbury, published by Oakwood Press.
The Isle of Wight Railways from 1923 Onwards by Maycock & Silsbury, published by Oakwood Press.
The Ventnor West Branch by Peter Paye published by Wild Swan Publications.
The Railway Magazine, various issues.
Isle of Wight County Press.
Various Internet Searches.

1 Ryde to Ventnor

Above: Taken on the same occasion as the frontispiece image, the Pier Tram shuttles its way to the Esplanade. The tramway pre-dates the rail link to the Pier Head by some considerable margin. Originally horse drawn, it opened in 1864 and extended to Ryde St Johns along the streets in 1871. It was later curtailed back to the Esplanade in 1880 when the railway was extended from St Johns by a joint LSWR/ LBSCR venture along the Pier, enabling direct access by rail to the boats. The tramway had the distinction of being powered by horse, then steam, electricity, and finally petrol driven railcars. The building seen above the tram is the Seagull Ballroom, now demolished. The tramway finally succumbed in 1969.

Opposite top: High summer at Ryde. At least two trains are ready for departure behind (L) No. 20 *Shanklin* and (Centre) No. 18 *Ningwood.* On the extreme right is No 24 *Calbourne.*

Opposite bottom: A Locomotive Club of Great Britain special working took place on 3 October 1965 to allow intrepid enthusiasts to experience a journey around the remaining network. Called the 'Vectis Farewell Tour', and so anticipating the demise of steam on the Island, the special was hauled as seen here by No. 24 *Calbourne* in BR black livery (now thankfully preserved on the IoW Steam Railway). She was later joined by No. 14 *Fishbourne* for double heading to Ventnor. The notice cautions persons of the presence of pile stumps and the dangers of passing under the structure.

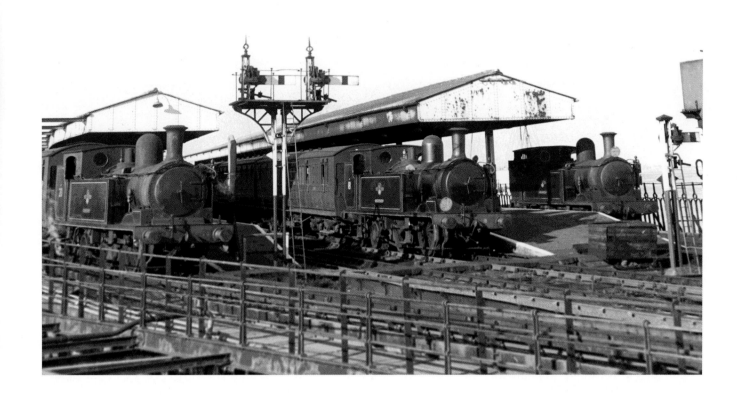

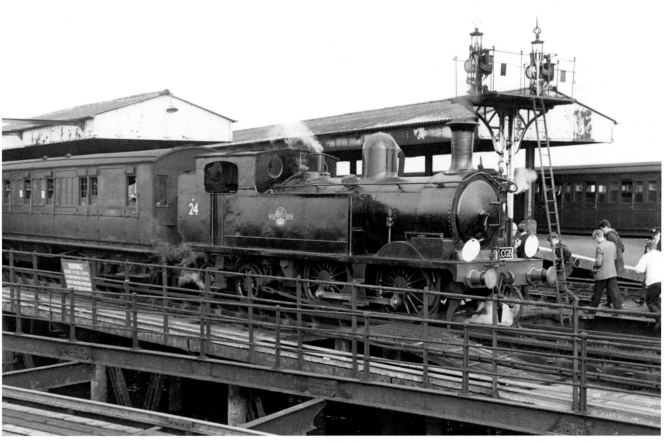

'O2' No. 20 *Shanklin* shuttles a solitary utility van from the Pier Head to the Esplanade station with parcels and mails. Passenger advance luggage was also handled by such movements in busier years. This view is almost certainly a summer Saturday transfer given the sheer volume of holiday traffic. The 1933 signalling diagram shows the signal box frame had 33 levers with just 5 spare.

'O2' class No. 14 *Fishbourne* departs the Pier Head with a Ventnor train. *Fishbourne* was one of the later survivors of the class, being finally scrapped in 1967. The LSWR design signal box provided a good view of train movements and the signalman was kept very busy especially on summer Saturdays. From 1922 the box additionally assumed control of all signals and points at Esplanade station. It closed on 5 May 1974 after re-signalling which included removal of the scissors crossover and semaphore signals.

'O2' class No. 35 *Freshwater* on a Ventnor bound train circa 1964. This engine was a later transfer from the mainland than her sisters, arriving in 1949. She was officially withdrawn in 1967 having been laid up for many months. The crossover seen here was only occasionally used, being controlled by the Pier Head signal box.

No. 20 *Shanklin* again at Ryde Esplanade with a train from Ventnor on a wet day around 1964. This image shows up well the bunker extension made on the Island based O2 class following experimental trials made in the early 1930s by Alistair McCloud. McCloud was effectively manager of the Island railways, appointed by the SR as Assistant to the Chief Mechanical Engineer in 1928. The family on the opposite platform are seemingly more interested in a Hovercraft movement.

Opposite: A train from Cowes departs Esplanade for the Pier Head hauled by 'O2' class No. 29 *Alverstone*. Crowds appear to be boarding the tram on their way to the ferry. *Alverstone* was included in the third batch of 'O2's sent to the Island in 1926 and was in active service here for exactly 40 years.

Above: No. 18 *Ningwood* awaits departure from Ryde Esplanade to Ryde St Johns around 1964. Most drivers had regular engines allocated to them during this time. *Ningwood* was favoured by well-known Driver Frankie Ash and his Fireman, Terry Hatcher. The necessary gradient to take the line down to clear Ryde Tunnel can clearly be seen. It was the entrance to Ryde Tunnel that was the scene of a fatality in 1954 when lengthman Dudley Saunders was hit by a train and killed whilst in the process of retrieving a crowbar. The tunnel was prone to flooding, disrupting train services, the line being below sea level at this point. Following the end of steam and introduction of low height tube stock the permanent way through the tunnel was raised to try and reduce the effect; unfortunately this has severely restricted the height of any stock able to operate, a restriction that persists to this day. Severe storms and extreme tides can still cause flooding of the tunnel in 2020.

| 1 | 2 | 3 | 4 |

1	Ryde Pier Head and Ventnor (all stations) also Newport and Freshwater
2	Cowes and Ventnor via Merstone
3	Goods Trains, Light Engines and Coaching Stock only Ryde Pier Head and Ryde St John's Road.
4	Newport and Ventnor West

Opposite top: Ningwood again this time at the third of the Ryde stations, Ryde St Johns on a Cowes bound train. This image was taken a few years earlier than the previous and denoted by the earlier 'lion & wheel' emblem on the tank side. The newer design appeared from 1956 onwards which helps to date this image. The roof of the Locomotive workshops appears above the train. The re-signalling that took place in May 1974 made reversible running between Pier Head and St Johns Road possible.

Opposite bottom: To prove it was also not always sunshine, in this latter days of steam view No. 32 *Bonchurch* is at Ryde St Johns on a three coach train in March 1962, the length of the train denoting the winter service is in operation. In pre-grouping days the road bridge marked the end of the LSWR/ LBSCR ownership and the start of the IWR/ IWCR metals. Escaping steam also suggests the maintenance of the locomotive fleet had been reduced as the future of the Island lines was becoming uncertain.

This page top: An excellent view of Ryde St Johns showing the facilities to good effect. Significant improvements seen here were made here by the SR from 1924 to 1930. Owing to cramped facilities on the south side of the station for engine stabling and maintenance, a new locomotive shed was constructed in the yard north of the road overbridge, the roof profile being seen here to the right of the signal box. This allowed for a re-organisation and expansion of the Works which included transferring some equipment and facilities from Newport, centralising maintenance facilities at Ryde. Further operational improvements, including doubling the line as far as Smallbrook, required the new signal box seen here. Opened in November 1928 it had 40 levers with 11 spare. In keeping with 'hand-me-downs' being sent to the Island, even this signal box structure was 'second-hand' having previously stood at Waterloo Junction.

This page bottom: A Newport/ Cowes train arrives at St Johns Road behind an unidentified engine. On the right hand side is the down loop line which was 600 feet long.

This page, top:
Above: The Works facilities are shown to good effect here. These included provision for locomotive, carriage and wagon workshops. Some then relatively new heavy lifting equipment, including a hoist and a 4-ton crane, can also be glimpsed here.

This page bottom; Lifting No. 33 *Bembridge* outside of the works and with the rear bogie removed for attention. Not only was the actual lifting undertaken outside, but the actual lifting hoist was also hand operated. (A rail mounted hand crane may also been seen in the background.) The removed bogie would be receiving attention inside the works. No. 33 is in Southern green livery but has acquired British Railways identification painted in the style of the old company.

Opposite top: Moving to the other side of the running lines to the locomotive shed we see O2 class No. 16 *Ventnor* and 26 *Whitwell* on 23 March 1962. *Ventnor* looks well coaled up ready for her next turn of duty. She survived to the end of steam being finally scrapped in 1967. *Whitwell* succumbed to the breakers' torch a year earlier.

Opposite bottom: Inside the two-road shed on 23 March 1962 showing the spacious interior. Four members of the class are present. No. 22 *Brading* in front of 25 *Godshill* and 14 *Fishbourne*. On the other road receiving some attention is 24 *Calbourne*. The shed was opened by the SR in 1930 replacing the original IWR one on the opposite side of the line

Opposite: 'E1' Class 0-6-0T No. 1 being dismantled at the rear of Ryde St Johns shed on 25 June 1957. Increasingly the Island based 'E1's were surplus to requirements with the contraction and eventual demise of goods workings and shunting at Medina Wharf. Originally four class 'E1's arrived on the Island (three in 1932 followed by one more the following year). They were joined by a solitary class 'E4' 0-6-2T in 1947 but the latter proved fairly unsuccessful and was shipped back to the mainland two years later.

Above; 'O2' No. 20 *Shanklin* at Ryde St Johns on 25 June 1957 still retaining the BR lion & wheel emblem. *Shanklin* was in one of the first batch of the class 'O2's delivered to the Island in 1923, still carrying her LSWR number 211. Along with her sister No. 19 *Osborne* she was lifted on to the railway at Ryde Pier Head, when the SR temporarily took loan of the Admiralty's Portsmouth-based floating crane. *Shanklin* lasted until the end of steam services, officially being withdrawn in 1967.

| 5 | 6 | 7 | 8 |

5   Ryde Pier Head and Cowes
6   Ryde Pier Head and Ventnor (not calling at all stations)
7   Brading and Bembridge
8   Shunting Engines

Opposite page: Amidst the detritus associated with any engine depot, an unidentified 'O2' peeps around the corner of the shed at Ryde. Coaling was undertaken by hand as was smokebox cleaning and the emptying of the ash pan and grate; hence the associated fire irons standing against the wall. The engine is clearly in steam as witness the wisp of steam from the top of the Westinghouse air-pump. The 'O2's on the Island were amongst the last steam engines operated by British Railways to retain this equipment and it was not unknown for the fireman to find it necessary to resort to climbing around the framing to give the pump a judicious 'clonk' with a spanner or hammer should it stop for no apparent reason. No pump meant no air, and no air pressure meant the brakes would start to drag on the train.

Right: Admiring glances at Ryde. The pump on this also unidentified engine has a cover attached.

Bottom: On what was a warm summers day, No. 24 *Calbourne* stands outside the shed whilst nearby piles of ash bear testimony to the work of countless firemen. The engine is coaled and so probably prepared for its next duty. A scene repeated thousands of times at both Ryde and Newport, until the latter closed and then Ryde too ceased to be a steam depot. No doubt the sudden lack of noise invariably associated with the steam shed was welcomed by the residents nearby. On the top of the left hand side tank may be seen the air reservoir connected to the Westinghouse pump.

Above: No. 18 *Ningwood* on a Ventnor service near Smallbrook Junction on 2 August 1958. Summer Saturdays during this period would see some 46 trains from Ryde to Ventnor testing line capacity to the limit. It was no surprise when the Southern Railway took the decision to double the line from Brading to Sandown to ease the pressure.

Opposite top: The daily parcels train nearing Smallbrook Junction hardly needing two locomotives but this is assumed here perhaps to avoid a light engine working. No. 24 *Calbourne* and 29 *Alverstone* being the engines in question. *Alverstone* was returned to the mainland briefly in 1947 for an extensive overhaul at Eastleigh possibly owing to the work required or perhaps a lack of capacity at Ryde Works at the time.

Bottom: No. 18 *Ningwood* is signalled for the Ventnor route as it passes the Smallbrook Junction down inner home signals; lever Nos. 18 (Ventnor line) and 17 (Newport) line. Although undated, the period is likely to be around 1949 with engine cleaning once again a regular undertaking. The single line section from Smallbrook Junction to Brading was worked by Train Staff which will be collected by the crew as the double line from Ryde ends and the engine passes the signal box.

Smallbrook Junction marked the end of the double track section from Ryde St Johns. Here we see No. 21 *Sandown* taking the Ventnor line on 2 August 1958. Next stop Brading. There was never a firm proposal for a station at Smallbrook as it would serve nowhere in particular, but occasional suggestions from the public for such did emerge from time to time over the years.

Above: Giving the impression of wrong line working, No. 30 *Shorwell* is heading a Ryde to Cowes train. In fact by the date of the photograph, 14 October 1961, Smallbrook Junction box had been switched out for the winter service and trains for Cowes and Ventnor respectively take the appropriate road at St Johns station with the section from St Johns to the divergence point operated as parallel single lines.

Opposite top: A Ventnor to Ryde service heads past Smallbrook Junction signal box on 26 June 1965 headed by No. 24 *Calbourne*. Smallbrook was said to be the most photographed signal box in the UK. Usually this was snapped from on board a train but this time the intrepid photographer has made his way along the footpath to reach the site. It has never had vehicular road access and still does not to this day; the new preservation steam railway station operating as an exchange point only on operating days. Smallbrook box had 24 levers with 4 spare.

Middle: Exchange made, No. 18 *Ningwood* speeds past Smallbrook for Ryde St Johns on a limited stop service from Ventnor on 24 July 1965. These types of services were introduced in the early 1930s in various forms, for example non-stop Ryde Pier Head to Sandown and non-stop Brading to Pier Head. Owing to traffic level restrictions (line capacity) they were never referred to as express services. By the 1950s, summer Saturdays saw a few of these "non-stop" services in the timetable mainly on the Ventnor line, some simply missing out Brading, and the intermediate Ryde stations.

Bottom: Driver Harry Watson gives the photographer a cheery smile as No. 21 *Sandown* passes Smallbrook Junction on a Ventnor service, 24 July 1965. *Sandown* was to survive another ten months, being withdrawn from service in May 1966.

Left: A final view of Smallbrook as the 1.40pm Ventnor to Ryde Pier Head crosses from the single line on to the double line section to complete its journey. The engine is again No. 18 *Ningwood.* When Smallbrook was switched out and the route operated as two parallel single lines to this point, the signal arms were removed, instruments disconnected, Nos. 11 and 13 facing points clipped and padlocked and the associated facing point locks fixed 'in'. The procedure was reversed again at the start of the following year's summer season.

No. 36 *Carisbrooke* near Brading around 1955. This was bridge number 38 built to accommodate double track as were others on this section anticipating a future need to lay an extra set of rails. The SR had in fact planned in 1924 to double from Sandown to Shanklin but this was later changed to just Sandown to Brading when it was found it would give greater operational flexibility. The engineering team probably regretted the change of plan as they hit all sorts of tricky soils and clays in the process of preparing the ground and the difficulties encountered delayed final opening until June 1927.

A Ventnor bound train arrives at Brading in the early 1950s hauled by namesake No. 22 *Brading*. The Bembridge branch has closed at this time, denoted by the removal of the signal arms (Nos. 4 & 5 in the frame) from the bracket signal at the end of the down platform. Ironically only a couple of years earlier BR had replaced an IWR lower quadrant signal with a modern bracket, as shewn on page 26. The Up starting signal is an LSWR type installed by the Southern Railway at the time the line from Brading to Sandown was doubled.

Left: No. 16 *Ventnor* having just left Brading for Ryde. Unusually the engine is facing north; nearly all trains having the engine facing south. There were no turntables on the island lines (two sector-plates yes; at Bembridge and at Ventnor) so at some stage No. 16 must have worked between Newport and Sandown in one direction only.

'Brading best kept station'. Brading, as can be seen here, won the best kept station award for Island stations in 1954, an annual competition similar to those run by most UK railway companies to encourage staff to work to the best of their ability. Separate competitions were operated for the 'best kept length' to encourage the permanent way gangs and 'best kept yards' to staff at goods stations/ yards. The actual bench seen here was moved to the winning station each year (see page 60) and now resides at the preservation centre at Haven Street.

A stunning view of Brading captured circa 1952/3 showing the station facilities to good effect. The Bembridge branch train is in the bay platform. When opened in 1864 Brading had one platform and was not a crossing place for passenger trains although a loop did exist to aid goods train movements. This changed in about 1870 when it was extended and a down platform constructed. The main station building remained largely unchanged until closure. On summer weekends certain Ryde bound trains did not call here hence the provision of co-acting arms for the up starting signal to enable it to be sighted from some distance away.

Opposite top: No. 20 Shanklin arrives at Brading. Notice the informative running-in board including the words 'Change for St Helens and Bembridge', this addition is missing from the later period view below. The Bembridge branch train is also signalled to leave the other side of the island platform but will not do so until any connections have been made. The previously referred to signals 4 & 5 are also present, No. 5 in the 'off' position. The Bembridge branch platform included an 'engine loop' to enable the branch engine to run round its train.

Opposite bottom: Busy times at Brading as trains cross on 28 August 1965 as captured by enthusiast Peter Gray's visit on that day. No. 17 Seaview waits with an up train for Ryde with an unidentified 'O2' on a Ventnor working. More than a decade has passed since the closure of the Bembridge branch but the formation is still largely intact. In the early days Brading was noted for the longevity of two of its serving station masters. Firstly George Corbett from 1870 until his death in 1912 still then in service aged 83, followed by William Wheway seeing out the IWR days.

Above: Brading signal box thankfully survives today and can be visited accompanied by helpful volunteers. It is now a protected Grade II listed building. Unlike many provided on the IWR which were of Saxby & Farmer design, Brading was of LSWR design and contained a Stevens frame of 30 levers with just two spare at the time the Bembridge branch was in operation. It dates from 1882. At the time double line working was in place to Sandown, 3-position open block working applied between the two stations. The significantly reduced point rodding and signal wires seen here clearly show the photograph was taken in later years. The corrugated hut on the left was used by the PW gang. The box closed in 1988 when the down line was removed through the station.

Opposite top: Now wearing smart BR lined black livery, No 22 *Brading* leaves Brading heading for Sandown in about 1952. A train for Bembridge can be seen waiting in the bay platform which helps to date the image as prior to the 1953 closure of the branch. The water tank is believed to date from the provision of the down platform in 1870. Being somewhat set back from the running line, it had an extended pipe to help the fireman in his task.

Opposite bottom: No. 22 *Brading* entering Brading with an up train for Ryde in the early 1960s. The double track section from Sandown opened in 1927 is apparent. The crossover was by this time little used but was maintained for any shunting requirements.

This page, top: Travelling light….. .an unidentified 'O2' makes her way light engine from Ryde St Johns to probably Sandown for a short working in the early 1960s. Prior to 1956 the opportunity to turn engines on the triangle formed by Ryde – Sandown – Merstone – Newport – Havenstreet – Ryde was utilised given the lack of turntables on the Island lines. It is known for example that the FYN Manning Wardle No. 1 was turned soon after arrival in 1913 so she could face Freshwater smoke box first.

This page, bottom: Leaving Brading for Sandown on 28 August 1965, No. 18 *Ningwood* pulls away on this double track section brought in by the SR in 1927 at a cost of £28,000 to cope with the pressure of increasing the timetable. *Ningwood* was originally built at Nine Elms in 1892 numbered 220 and transferred to the Island in 1930. Lovingly cared for by her regular driver Frank Ash she became the victim of a catastrophic boiler failure in 1965 shortly after this photo was taken so putting an end to her life. She was cannibalised for spares at Ryde St Johns and later her remaining carcass was towed to Newport, eventually being moved again to Cement Mills siding and broken up there by HP Jolliffe of Somerton in January 1967.

A panoramic view of Sandown looking towards Brading in BR days. On the left, platform three was used by trains to and from Newport via Merstone. The lofty signal box perched above the island platform canopy provided the signalman with an excellent sighting for train movements. It contained 32 levers in use and dates from 1893 as does the platform canopy. Two stern warning signs attempted to ensure would be passengers did not exit or enter the station from the occupation crossing.

In 1880 a refreshment room licence was granted to William Henry Clarke and it became an important venue where chess tournaments took place in the dining room. Station Master Mark Gregory was thought to be a keen chess enthusiast. He retired in March 1910 but it is not known if the chess activities continued after his departure.

WARNING
PASSENGERS
ARE STRICTLY
FORBIDDEN
TO ENTER THE
STATION
THIS WAY

Above: The substantial looking station building was deceptive in that the station master's living accommodation was incorporated as part of it which ended up restricting the space for station facilities. There was no porters' room and the ladies' waiting room was soon sacrificed to provide a station master's office. It was soon realised enlarging the building was unavoidable and the 1871 single storey extension can be seen here nearest the camera. Further enhancement came when the IWR extended both platforms by some 30 feet around 1915 to accommodate longer trains. The station was some distance from the town and even further from the seafront, thus in the early days the provision of horse-drawn taxis was a helpful convenience. The station was known as '*Sandown Junction*' from when the IWNJR line opened in 1864 but reverted to plain Sandown in later years. When the IWR had first opened between Ryde & Shanklin in 1864 its administrative offices were based at Sandown but these soon moved to Ryde.

Right: 'O2' class No. 36 *Carisbrooke* at Sandown about to set off for Ventnor in the early 1950s. This engine was a later addition to the fleet shipped to the Island in 1949 along with sister engine No. 35 *Freshwater*. As there was a footpath running parallel to the line and an adjacent occupation crossing, it was felt an access warning sign was necessary.

Above: This image portrays a late 1950s view of Sandown station after the closure of the line to Newport via Merstone. The rails were removed about 1958 and the track bed of this route was sold to the Island County Council in 1961. The run-round loop for the former IWC platform was relatively short at 344 feet. The sidings seen here could hold up to 57 wagons. Although access was now severed at the Shanklin end, these were still available to store empty or condemned stock if required.

Opposite top: An unidentified 'O2' enters Sandown with a Ryde bound train. The occupation crossing just south of the station provided access to the allotments and an adjacent farm track. When opened the station would have been in a somewhat rural location a little distance away from the population it was meant to serve, but over the years development of the town extended towards the railway.

Opposite bottom; 'O2' No. 30 *Shorwell* at Sandown on a Newport via Merstone train circa 1954. Platform three remained the platform for Newport departures right from IWNJR days and operation by the IWCR until the 1956 closure of this route, necessitated by the track layout. A Ventnor bound train can be seen in the background providing a connection for Shanklin, Wroxall and Ventnor. Prior to the September 1952 closure of the Ventnor West branch, passengers originating from Newport for Ventnor could have changed at Merstone and travelled to Ventnor West but few did, preferring the IWR route, despite the stunning sea views on offer from emergence at High Hat tunnel through St Lawrence to the West station. *Shorwell* was scrapped in 1965.

Left: A Ryde bound train enters Sandown behind an unidentified 'O2' but believed to be No. 26 *Whitwell*. Note the fireman about to surrender the Shanklin – Sandown tablet. A plethora of notices can be seen in the interests of protecting the public, the occupation crossing access required making this somewhat apparent. On the down side, a 'Shunt Ahead' arm was added to the down starting signal post in June 1953, this allowed the engine of a 'short section' service terminating at Sandown to run forward into the section solely for the purpose of reaching the end of the loop and so be able to run round.

Bottom: The station forecourt at Sandown approached from the town. Of note is the Southern Railway sign although this image is well into BR days, there was never really a rush on the Island to change these. The British Road Services lorry will be taking onward parcels to delivery around the immediate area. The station was inconveniently located quite some distance from both the town and the beach, the line passing around the back of the town. The SR undertook a number of improvements in 1938 including lengthening the platforms further (they had already been extended in 1915) and enlarging the station building. These included provision of new toilets and allowed changes to the booking hall, freeing up space.

Top: Here we have No. 27 *Merstone* leaving Sandown on a Ventnor service. The number three on display is the crew roster number. We have two things in the image which help us date the photograph to 1956 or early 1957. Access to platform 3 has been severed indicating it is after the closure of the line via Merstone, whilst the earlier BR emblem suggests it can't be beyond the following year.

Bottom: Not sure if this sort of public access would be permitted in these days of health & safety intolerance, but in the early 1950s it was a case of just 'Stop, Look and Listen' before crossing the line - and people did just that. However this was a *bona fide* public crossing immediately south of Sandown station and here a family and others wait either side of the line for the passing of No. 22 *Brading* on a Ventnor bound train.

Above: The approaches to Shanklin station from the north and looking south to Wroxall. Shanklin has been the terminus of the line twice in fact. The first occasion was when the section of the IWR opened to the station in 1864 and it remained a terminus until 1866 when the Ventnor extension opened and the second (up) platform was added. It reverted to a terminus again a century later in 1966 after the loss of Ventnor to the railway network and remains so until this day. Back in 1866, temporary facilities were provided for locomotives and a carriage shed also provided, both lasting until through workings to Ventnor commenced when the second platform was added. An early style ground signal can be seen controlling exit from the yard siding to the down loop. As this had a yellow arm it could be passed at 'on' for shunting into the goods shed siding. The jib of the yard crane is visible at the end loading dock. The first station master at Shanklin was James Sulley, appointed in 1865, replaced a few years later in 1871 by George Humby.

Opposite top: Looking towards Wroxall in the late 1950s. The main station building was conveniently on the town side of the station and accommodation consisted of a two-storey station master's house topped by an attractive turret, waiting rooms and offices being provided on each side. The 1870s saw further improvements to facilities and siding accommodation. Despite this, accommodation was cramped in later years as traffic volumes grew and the SR considered a complete rebuild but baulked somewhat at the cost instead tinkering around with available space instead. The siding leading off the end of the up platform led to the town gas works and a simple covered structure may just be seen in the distance where coal wagons would be left for handling into the retorts.

Opposite bottom: The station forecourt with a splendid selection of 1950s and earlier cars on display. The Southern Railway sign survived well into BR days as they did at many Island stations. To the right can be seen the canopies erected over the loading dock platform, these were added in 1935 to provide protection particularly for handling passenger luggage as a significant amount was sent on in advance under the PLA (Passengers Luggage in Advance) system.

Opposite top; A superb view of a busy Shanklin with No. 31 *Chale* heading away on a Ryde bound train in the early 1950s. The head code denotes this is a limited stop service. The origins of these go back to IWR days when many respiratory invalids were taken from Ryde to Ventnor bound for the TB Hospital and recuperation.

Opposite bottom: From the same vantage point, and again with the opposite direction Ventnor bound train already in the down platform, the section to Sandown was thus clear for No. 22 *Brading* to pull away from Shanklin in the early 1950s on a limited stop service, possibly missing out Brading and Ryde St Johns. The two vans in the loading dock siding are or were possibly carrying PLA (Passenger Luggage in Advance). The canopy over the dock platform (the edge of which is seen here) was erected in 1935 to facilitate the growth and popularity of this system.

Above: The approaches to Shanklin station from Sandown seen here in the 1950s. Only one platform originally existed when the station functioned as a temporary terminus until the line opened to Ventnor. The siding accommodation seen here provided for coal traffic and a loading dock. Various improvements and extensions to accommodation for both passenger and goods were undertaken at times between 1872 and 1878, including the second platform. Signalling and interlocking improvements were made in 1891 including the provision of a 20 lever signal box (having two spare levers, Nos 5 and 16) at the south end seen in the distance in this image below the signal gantry. The gantry to allow the down home signal to be placed high above the running line was necessary for sighting purposes. During his tenure in office (1871 – 1913) Station Master George Humby would have witnessed all these changes.

Left: A moment of relaxation at Shanklin around 1964 for the engine crew as No. 18 *Ningwood* awaits an up train to arrive before proceeding to Ventnor. The ground signal seen here controls access to the gas works siding. Note the homing pigeon baskets on the opposite platform; this service for fanciers was a relatively common feature at certain stations across the UK at this time and is well remembered by the author at his then home station. The railway provided both for the transport of and subsequent release of the birds at a predetermined time.

Bottom: Clearly it was a wet day in Shanklin on 28 March 1962 as No. 31 *Chale* arrives with the 3:25pm train from Ryde. The shorter three carriage train is typical of the winter timetable service. Shanklin was the scene of an unfortunate fatality in 1928 when permanent way gang member Fred Calloway was killed falling under a moving train.

Right: Nearing the end of steam, The Locomotive Club of Great Britain (LCGB) organised a special enthusiast working which took place on 3 October 1965 travelling over the few lines still open. No. 24 *Calbourne* being the main charge for the day, being joined by No. 14 *Fishbourne* for double-heading the trip to Ventnor. Here at Shanklin the train stopped on the return from Ventnor for photo opportunities interestingly using the down platform with the up platform rammed with enthusiasts. The engines were then detached and ran through the up platform stopping just clear whilst many cameras were busy snapping away. Ominously the conductor rails are already in place, a portent of things to come.

Bottom: Shanklin, on the last day of steam services, on 31 December 1966 with No. 14 *Fishbourne* adorned for the occasion with a farewell to steam wreath and a headboard replacing the normal headcode disk. By this time of course the line onward to Ventnor had been closed (17 April 1966) so this was the end of the line, just as it had been before in the 1860s. The crowds coming from far and wide to get a last look at steam were huge with trains throughout the day being seriously overcrowded. *Fishbourne* had the honour of hauling the last service from Ryde to Shanklin and back, it was reported that some 500 people were packed into every available carriage space.

Above: Leaving Shanklin for Wroxall the line climbed across Apse Heath at a gradient of some 1 in 70 for a mile and a quarter. Here we see No. 33 *Bembridge* 'in the collar' on a Ventnor bound train breasting the bank around 1954. The shallow cutting is predominantly sand, appropriately named Sand Cutting. In the far background is Brading Down.

Opposite: In Sand Cutting No. 20 *Shanklin* works a Ryde to Ventnor service passing under one of several bridges on this section. The permanent way is looking well maintained in this circa 1954 image.

Opposite top: An unidentified 'O2' passes the weed strewn up siding at Wroxall on the approach to the station. Access to this was obtained by inserting the Shanklin – Wroxall train staff into the ground frame although from the look of the rails this has not been necessary for some time.

Opposite bottom: The driver of No. 27 *Merstone* awaits right away from the guard on a sunny day in the mid-1950s. The Starting signal is interesting in that it has an LCDR style finial leading to suggestions that this and other signals at Wroxall were second hand originating on that line possibly from Cannon Street. The Porter/ Signalman looks to be relaxed in the sun passing the time of day with the engine crew. *Merstone* was the last 'O2' to be steamed at Newport on 18 April 1967 when she hauled her sister engines to Freshwater Yard, Newport, for cutting up.

Above: A classic view of Wroxall station taken in a quiet moment. Wroxall originally had a single platform and did not gain its passing loop until the SR improvements of 1924. With the second platform it was felt necessary to provide a footbridge although curiously this was not mentioned as a requirement in the Board of Trade inspection made somewhat late in 1926. It was soon realised by the SR that they could do this on the cheap by dismantling the one at Dean Crossing on the Ventnor West branch and erecting it at Wroxall. It would certainly receive more footfall here as given the train service on the Ventnor West line it was an unnecessary luxury where it was. Interestingly a signal box to control the new signals and loop points was not provided, the lever frame and staff instruments being located in the booking office instead. The station master at this time was Thomas Chiverton who was appointed in 1918.

Left: Crossing trains at Wroxall. At peak times during the holiday season it was not unknown for the crossing places at Shanklin and Wroxall to be in use simultaneously whilst trains would also likely pass between Brading and Sandown and Ryde and Smallbrook. A case of shoe-horning the holiday service into the available infrastructure. The staff were well-versed in such activities although it only took a late running service or worse still an engine failure to throw all into chaos. At Wroxall the up and down services are passing without incident; ten minutes of feverish activity for the station staff and signalman followed by inactivity before the process was repeated once more - many times during the day. No *17 Seaview is* waiting the arrival of No. 21 *Sandown* in the late afternoon of the summer service. In the distance it is just possible to make out the six masts of the former WW2 Ventnor Radar Station the remaining towers from which were finally pulled down in 1957.

Bottom; No. 25 *Godshill* leaving Wroxall on a down train on 28 March 1962. *Godshill* was in her last year of service, being withdrawn in 1963. In the distance under the overbridge some assorted wagons can be seen on the siding at the north end of the station which served the Flux bacon factory.

Above: Relaying work underway on 28 March 1962 as the 10:52am train from Ventnor passes the permanent way gang, hauled by No. 31 *Chale*. It was a 1 in 88 down gradient now dropping most of the way to Wroxall. Ventnor tunnel was 1,312 yards long, passing deep under St Boniface Down. The summit of the line at 300 feet above sea level occurred just before the tunnel more or less where the photographer is positioned, the line then falling at 1 in 173 through the tunnel to Ventnor station. *Chale* had an unlucky end as she was almost saved from the scrapyard in May 1967 along with her more fortunate sister *Calbourne*, but a last minute attempt failed as cutting up had already commenced beyond economic viability.

Right; A Ryde train leaving the tunnel. The permanent way hut is a former wagon body grounded and serving a new use. The engine is No. 17 *Seaview* on the 3.40pm from Ventnor to Pier Head.

Above: The dramatic setting of Ventnor station has always made it a favourite location for railway enthusiasts, modellers and photographers. The IWR took over the benefit of using what had been a quarry for their station albeit still high above the town and tersely described by the Chairman of the rival IWCR as 'half-way up a mountain' at the time of the opening of their line to Ventnor Town (later West) in 1900. Despite this inconvenience passengers always seemed to prefer to arrive here and the IWCR line failed to be a serious competitor. In the early days the wealthy would have their horse drawn carriages waiting for them to arrive, lesser mortals could avail themselves especially post-war by intrepid young boys offering to take passengers' luggage to their hotel on carts and prams, no doubt being rewarded with a 6d or two.

Opposite top: No. 27 *Merstone* has run around her train in the station and is poised to run back on the correct road to couple up for the return journey to Ryde. The signalman has the train staff ready for the driver to collect as he moves forward. This was only possible as there was not another incoming service due before departure time. The photograph dates from the mid-1950s. Key-token working to Wroxall replaced the train staff from 18 June 1957.

Opposite bottom; The Ventnor Signalman (thought to be Alec Widger) poses for the photographer sometime in the 1950s. Ventnor Signal box was a Saxby & Farmer design containing 17 levers with 2 spare as shown on the 1933 diagram. Lingering smoke from the tunnel could cause a problem for sighting of signals and drivers had to be careful. However this could not be blamed for a signalman error in July 1937 when a train was signalled to enter platform one, already occupied by another train. Fortunately the driver was alert and pulled up in time to avoid collision. Shunting into the tunnel was also commonplace, sometimes involving an engine and coaches. To assist movements in the gloom, three electric shunting bells were provided; the first for an engine and two coaches 54 yards inside, the next for an engine with three or four coaches at 93 yards and finally a further bell for five and six coach trains at 132 yards into the darkness. These were in use by at least 1948.

Opposite top: Looking towards the end of the line an unidentified 'O2' is in the process of running around a recently arrived train. Originally a sector plate was provided as the engine release as a space saver, but this was later replaced by a more conventional headshunt. The site had its space restrictions which may have accounted for the double platform face, but passenger accommodation proved sufficient even for busy summer Saturdays. Equally the goods yard compromised with a layout including some difficult pointwork. Shunting moves were therefore potentially risky, including reversing into the tunnel, and necessitated special instructions in the Company's rule book. The sidings were rearranged in 1933 to accommodate bogie carriages. The caves to the right were a legacy of the quarrying activity prior to the arrival of the railway and these were rented out to coal merchants and other traders. A substantial goods shed was provided with a distinctive arched roof seen here on the left.

Opposite bottom: No. 27 *Merstone* takes water having recently arrived from Ryde. The curve in the retaining wall on the left is a legacy of the sector plate release long removed. The GPO Telephone Box was apparently well used right up until closure of the station in 1966. A spare set of coaching stock can be seen stabled in the yard. Unlike many of the intermediate stations, strangely Ventnor was not originally provided with a station master's house until it was decided by the IWR Directors to do so in 1915. It is thought a property was rented elsewhere prior to this date to accommodate long-time S/M William Wetherwick and his successor.

Above: The classic view of Ventnor from the Downs, the sheer height looking down always giving the impression of a model. The awkward position of the station relevant to the town led to several plans to overcome this, the most serious in 1898 to link the two by way of a funicular railway dropping on a gradient of one in four at its steepest to the seafront behind the Mill Bay Inn. The IWR itself did consider building a new route as early as 1865 even before the original planned one opened in 1866. This would have branched off the planned line north of the existing tunnel, dropping steeply and emerging under Newport Road (now Mitchell Avenue), curving to the left to a new station fronting St Boniface Road. Although this would have been far more convenient than a station 294 feet above sea level, it was extremely costly and got no further than an aspiration in some Directors' minds.

Opposite top: No. 17 *Seaview,* on the inner side of the island platform at Ventnor, awaits departure to Ryde sometime around 1955. *Seaview* arrived on the Island in 1930 along with her sister *Ningwood* as part of the continuing numbers of the class sent over by the SR. She survived until the end of steam in 1966, being scrapped the following year. To aid the platform staff at Ventnor, in 1938 a bell code system was introduced operated from the signal box so as to inform them into which platform a train was going to arrive.

Opposite bottom: Anticipating contraction of the Island railways and the end of steam, a special Locomotive Club of Great Britain working occurred on 3 October 1963 entitled *The Vectis Rail Tour* utilising both No. 24 *Calbourne* and No. 14 *Fishbourne*, the latter double-heading for part of the tour only. All the then opened lines were visited with stopovers like here at Ventnor for enthusiasts and photographers to get their fix. In this view *Fishbourne* is out of shot at the front of the train with a clean *Calbourne* as the train engine coupled to the carriage set. Meanwhile No. 28 *Ashey* sits in the yard having arrived on a normal service train.

Above: About to leave Ventnor on 28 August 1965 the crew of No. 17 *Seaview* chat to the guard prior to departure. The problem encountered by engine crews with smoke lingering in the tunnel is apparent in this image hence the value of the shunting bells referred to earlier. The end of train services to Ventnor came on 17 April 1966 cutting off the town from railway connection for ever. No. 14 *Fishbourne* had the care of the last departure at 8:30pm on that sad Sunday evening. Among the staff made redundant at the station was signalman Alec Widger who had spent virtually all his railway career at Ventnor, starting at Ventnor West in 1930.

2 Smallbrook Junction to Cowes

Above: Back to Smallbrook Junction and here we have a Ryde to Cowes summer service as indicated by signal number 17 pulled off by Signalman Spears on 26 June 1965. An accessible footpath towards Smallbrook Junction led off a minor road bridge not visible here but located a short distance behind the last carriage.

Left: Believed to have been taken on the Newport / Cowes line near to Smallbrook Junction; the driver's eye view from the cab of an unidentified 'O2' taken sometime in the early 1960s. The photographer is unknown but either a fortunate enthusiast riding on the footplate or perhaps a keen crew member.

Top: Coming off the Cowes line at Smallbrook Junction we have No. 25 *Godshill* bound for Ryde. The presence of the arm on the signal indicates this is a summer service, possibly circa 1949.

Bottom: At the same location, this time it is No. 3 *Ryde* with what could well be coal for the depot. Most coal supplies for the Island were landed at Medina Wharf with the 'E1' class usually in charge of these workings until their demise. Again a summer time working, possibly taken on the same day.

Opposite top: Ashey was the first station reached from the junction at Smallbrook on the former IWCR route to Newport opened in 1875. The station building was very substantial for such a small station, possibly doffing a cap to Sir Henry Oglander of Nunwell who sold much of his land to the railway or possibly anticipating growth in the race going fraternity. The photograph gives the impression that the station is closed but the economies made in both the 1920s and 1960s led initially to the conversion of the passing loop serving the down platform into a siding in 1926 (trains now passed at the newly rebuilt Haven Street instead) and later in 1961 to remove it altogether and slew the running line to use the down platform only. The station became unmanned in 1926 and the building was let out for rent for many years following these changes but boarded up by the time of this photograph. It was eventually sold off by BR and with various owner improvements is now a delightful domestic dwelling and remains in this form today. Ashey was provided with a siding and until 1907 had a spur off this which led to a quarry (later cut back when the quarry closed). It also served the racecourse which opened in 1882, the siding conveniently running alongside the course. Special race trains arrived and departed from Ashey when meetings were held. The shortened siding leading to the racecourse was removed in 1927. The racecourse grandstand went up in flames three years later putting an end to racing. Here No 35. *Freshwater* pauses en route to Newport. Note the more decorative tops than usually provided on the concrete nameboard posts.

Opposite bottom: An unidentified O2 arrives at the replacement platform at Ashey. Despite the apparent lack of passengers, Ashey was however a popular station for walkers and ramblers to start or finish their activities. Little evidence of the siding that once existed here remains with the thick undergrowth. It was a fairly barren and sometimes exposed windswept spot. In the days when the quarry and siding were fully in use it was said the staff would wrap themselves in coal sacks in mid-winter to keep warm.

Below: It's my Mother's fault too! Like the infant in the pram I was always being taken to see the trains from an early age and maybe he was instilled with the love of railways through his life as well. This is a scene at Haven Street that fortunately can almost be replicated today thanks to the efforts of the Steam Heritage line. Here No. 27 *Merstone* enters the station with a train for Cowes on 22 August 1965 whilst No.14 *Fishbourne* waits with a Ryde bound up train. The latter engine in particular reflects the effort Island loco crews put in to keep their engines clean at a time when generally many steam locomotives in the UK were starting to look more unkempt. The signalman is about to take the Smallbrook Junction – Haven Street section tablet from the crew of *Merstone*.

Opposite top: Haven Street before the preservationists moved in to transform the station into its current status as one of the most popular tourist destinations on the Island. The original station building provided here was constructed in wood and was very different from what we see both here in this view and today. We are fortunate in that taking a look at the new station at Wootton offers us sight of a replica of what Haven Street used to be. Haven Street as seen here represents the new station constructed by the SR in 1926. The crossing loop was opened in July of that year rendering the crossing of trains at Ashey obsolete; the section then becoming Smallbrook – Haven Street (Ryde St Johns – Haven Street when Smallbrook switched out). The brick station building contained an integral signal box. The building on the left was part of a gas works established in 1886 for which a siding was added at that time facing up trains. The gas works closed circa 1920 but the siding was retained and used to handle coal traffic.

Opposite bottom: No. 14 *Fishbourne* again at Haven Street on 22 August 1965 having arrived from Newport. The 1926 station building was a vast improvement on the sparse accommodation that existed before that date. A waiting room, ladies' waiting room, toilets and an interlinked booking office and signal box were contained within the structure. The frame had 16 levers with 3 spare at the time of opening.

This page: The bench we saw earlier at Brading (page 26) and clearly well travelled in the interim. The Southern Railway encouraged competition between stations which were placed into specific groups. The idea being that staff would work to present a favorable appearance, station gardens being a feature which featured highly when the day of inspection occurred. The winning station would be featured in the staff magazine and a small cash prize awarded to the local station master to be used to buy further embellishments for the location.

Opposite top: The remains of Wootton station (basically just the platform!) are passed by No. 16 *Ventnor* on 29 August 1965, some 12 years after closure. Maintenance of the station environs was persistently difficult with ground slippages not helped by the blue slipper clay soils. It was almost certainly a factor in the decision to close it in 1953. The station facilities consisted of a booking office, waiting room and a signal box controlling signals. A siding was put in on the other side of the bridge in 1898 controlled by a small ground frame unlocked by the train staff. The formation of this after closure in 1966 proving useful for the new station constructed by the Heritage Steam Railway on this side of the bridge. Around 1907 an arch of the three arch road bridge was bricked in to form a replacement booking office, it is thought the platform was extended at the same time. It is likely the signal box was closed in 1912 when Wootton ceased to be a block post and the signals removed, the next station, Whippingham, then assuming this function.

Opposite bottom: Whippingham was a station totally out of scale to the population it served. It was built and opened in 1875 on a grander scale owing to the fact it was the nearest station to Osborne House (two and a half miles away) although it was not provided with a royal waiting room. It is known that visitors to the royal estate used the station, but whether Queen Victoria did is another matter. It was also a considerable distance from Whippingham village (nearly three miles) and really served nowhere in particular so it was no surprise that it closed in September 1953 along with Wootton (the latter for different reasons). It was operationally useful as it had a 455 foot passing loop from 1912 lasting until 1956. An 11 lever frame was located in the booking office with the provision of a down platform including a waiting shelter believed to have previously been a signal box elsewhere. The platforms were considerably shortened by BR soon after nationalisation, which given the imminent 1953 closure seems now a waste of resources.

Below: An unusual view taken from a train on the Sandown line in the early 1950s. This shows the end of the Ryde section of the viaduct and the line curving away towards the short (73 yard) tunnel under Fairlee Road. The formation today is buried until the slip road off the dual carriageway. Part of the other end of the tunnel exists today as a footpath.

Left: No. 32 *Bonchurch* leaves Newport for Ryde on the viaducts south of the station. Having passed over the Medina basin bridge and taken the sharp curve restricted to 10mph (as the sign shows) the train is at the point where the viaducts split, with the line to Ryde taking a left curve and the Sandown line to the right. Note the signal arms on the gantry are slightly angled for sighting purposes for the engine crews approaching Newport. This view dates from about 1956 as looking at the tops of the rails on the Sandown line they don't appear much traffic has passed over them recently and indeed the line may have recently closed.

Bottom: A train from Ryde rounds the 10mph restricted curve approaching Newport station in the mid-1950s. The Fireman is about to pass over the single line tablet to the signalman at Newport South box. The Sandown line on the right has already closed. The tall building on the left is the Retort House dating from 1937, part of the gas works originally established on this site in 1851. The gas works closed in the 1970s when a cross Solent gas main was opened supplying North Sea gas across the Island and the local works closed. The retort house was eventually demolished and the land cleared. The Riverside Centre and its car park are now on this site. The little shed seen on the right at the foot of the viaduct contained the mechanism for operating the quay swing bridge.

Spotters perhaps - yes there were some on the Island as well - but with no obvious note books visible. Perhaps they are waiting a delayed train from Cowes, certainly there may be something due as No. 35 Freshwater has the signal against it and so is unable to proceed further north for the present.

Displaying the Cowes to Ventnor via Merstone headcode (or vice-versa), No 22 *Brading* is seen at Newport. As per the mainland, Isle of Wight trains displayed head code discs according to the route being taken rather than the type of train and whilst the intensity of services was never that of say the London suburban area it did assist signalmen and platform staff in identifying workings should there be a delay or out of course running. We may doubt slightly the actual headcode displayed as from the fashions the period of the photograph would appear to relate more to the 1960s than prior to 1956 when the Merstone route had closed.

This page, 'E1's at Newport.

Top: No. 3 *Ryde* outside the two-road engine shed opened by the IWCR in 1891. Extensive workshops were also provided as part of this development, requiring the 1875 line dropping down to the Quay to be closed and much of the formation filled in. Workshop facilities were well provided and included a machine and fitting shop, smithy, wheel turning machine, forges, paint & carpenters' shop and a steam hammer, all machines believed to be purchased second-hand from the mainland.

Middle: Class 'E1' 0-6-0T No. 4 *Wroxall* in the yard at Newport. *Wroxall* was one of four E1 class engines shipped to the Island (3 in 1932, joined by *Wroxall* in 1933) predominantly for goods workings. With the decline in this type of traffic they were becoming surplus to requirements by the late 1950s and No. 4 was the last to be withdrawn in 1960. Behind the engine can be seen the roof profile of the Electricity Station, one of the very few reminders of this area of Newport surviving today, albeit disused and in a very dilapidated state.

Class 'E1' No. 1 *Medina* shunting a carriage in Newport yard around 1955. The Shunter is saving himself a walk by hitching a ride on the cab steps. The two-road engine shed was constructed in wood and opened on 2 February 1891. *Medina* was withdrawn in June 1957, the photo on page 16 shows her being cut up at Ryde. The last of her sisters ceased work in 1960 reflecting the reduction in goods workings required on the Island.

This page, 'O2's at Newport.

Top: Resplendent in Southern green livery but with nationalisation ownership displayed on the side tanks, No. 29 *Alverstone* is in light steam and possibly only recently overhauled. The single headcode disc (from Newport) indicated a Freshwater train and it may well be the engine was being made ready for such a working.

Middle: Namesake, No. 34 *Newport* under the lifting gantry at Newport shed. The photographer comments a grey patch had been painted on the tankside so obliterating the former 'Southern' wording. No. 34 together with No. 23 *Totland* were the first two casualties of the Island 'O2' class, both withdrawn in August 1955 partly because the closures already wrought had reduced the need for so many locomotives.

Bottom: No. 35 *Freshwater* shunting loco coal wagons at the coal platform around 1953. This facility dates from the opening of the new two-road engine shed. In the early years of the 20th century the goods sidings at Newport were proving woefully inadequate to handle the growing traffic levels and the significant marshalling of goods vehicles necessary given the configuration of the Island rail network. Some rearrangement took place to improve matters, necessitating amongst other things the demolition of the carriage shed. In this view the distinctive end roof profile of the Electricity Power Station can be seen in the background between the locomotive and the wagon.

Opposite top: No. 29 *Alverstone* takes water as she waits for departure to Cowes around 1962. The line to Freshwater curves away on the left, now truncated to 'Newport Freshwater Yard' only. Newport North signal box seen here had 36 levers and was supplied by the Railway Signal Company. It was proposed in the 1860s to provide a station at Dodnor, a short distance from Newport to serve Parkhurst, but this was not proceeded with.

Bottom: Here we have a view of No. 30 *Shorwell* stood outside the North signal box with the headcode applicable for a Ryde - Cowes working but clearly without its train. Some interesting variations for the dolls as well on the gantry; that furthest away of timber whilst the other three are lattice. All are also lower quadrant arms although these were changed to upper quadrant fittings in later years. The man on the post appears not to be a railwayman which perhaps explains the guilty look! On the left is the corner of Newport North signal box, renamed Newport 'B' in 1950. With the closure of the direct line to Sandown, the former South ('A') signal box had its workload reduced and so it was no real surprise when it was closed and 'B' renamed simply 'Newport' taking over all the work at the station from 23 March 1958.

Above: Perhaps the photographer did not realise at the time but he captured a rare beast indeed. This is the solitary former LBSCR class 'E4' 0-6-2T sent to the Island in February 1947 seen here in the shed yard at Newport. At the time the 'O2's were reported as being hard pressed to maintain schedules at peak holiday times and a larger engine was deemed necessary. At the same time consideration was being given to pull-push working between Ryde and Ventnor but no trials as such were ever carried out. To comply with the limited Island loading gauge a shorter chimney and modifications to the footsteps were made although in practice it was found the running plate came into contact with the curved platforms at Cowes. Trials were made over all the Island lines but no advantage was found over the existing engines, indeed and not surprisingly considering its larger size, it used more coal and water than an 'O2' and consequently No. 2510 (the engine was never renumbered for Island use) languished at Newport as 'spare engine' sometimes working services to Freshwater or being used on ballast duties. It was returned to the mainland in April 1949 still carrying her SR number. She was eventually scrapped in 1962.

Opposite top: No. 1 *Medina* in Newport yard having made up a mixed train which it will now take to Ryde. It is almost certain this service ran without passengers, the two coaches marshalled at the front to assist with braking.

Opposite bottom; Arrival from Cowes in the early 1960s hauled by No. 29 *Alverstone*. A couple of enthusiastic individuals can be seen leaning out of the first carriage clearly enjoying their trip. When *Alverstone* first arrived on the Island in 1926 she had a Drummond pattern boiler but clearly by the time of this photograph this had been substituted for the Adams type now fitted. *Alverstone* was withdrawn from service in 1966. The lofty bracket signal for arriving trains by the North signal box carries two arms but formally carried four before the closure of the line to Freshwater. Its structure, located for sighting purposes, required a number of guide wires for stability.

Top: A case of *Newport* at Newport as No. 34 enters the station from Cowes. Taken circa 1949 this shows the engine in the first BR livery with 'British Railways' in full on the tank side. Only sent to the Island in 1947 her stay was brief as she was withdrawn in 1955. Newport North signal box is just visible on the extreme left and the line to Freshwater curves away bottom left in this image. This arrangement facing Cowes, dating from the opening of the FYN, was awkward and operationally tedious with reversals in and out of the station to gain onward journey.

Middle: No. 22 *Brading* (right) on a Cowes service and No. 28 *Ashey* shunting on the left. Signalling rationalisation is apparent with the loss of the dolls and arms on the gantry ahead of the engine consequent upon the closure of the Freshwater line. (Compare with the view opposite top.)

Bottom: Busy times at Newport North. Arriving is No. 34 *Newport* on a service to Sandown via Merstone, whilst awaiting departure for Cowes is No. 31 *Chale* with a train from Ryde. To the right are the extensive sidings at Newport referred to earlier.

Newport North with No. 30 *Shorwell* in charge of the 3.30pm train from Sandown to Cowes. This will have been the seventh stop for the train since departure. On the right in the immediate foreground is what was known as the 'branch siding' running behind Newport North signal box and parallel to the Freshwater branch. The 'O2' standing in the Down bay is not identified.

A busy time at the south end of Newport around 1950 with sister engines Nos. 34 *Newport* and 27 *Merstone.* Judging by the head code *Newport* looks to have arrived on a Freshwater service. *Merstone* is about to head for Sandown via Blackwater. Although both engines appear rather grubby, they reflect the transition from the malachite green livery with British Railways spelt in full on No. 34 compared to the lined black and lion & wheel emblem on the tank sides of No. 27.

Three final views of Newport. Top left: The old water tank (later replaced) at the shed and recorded almost silhouetted into the afternoon sky. Again the decorative iron work is apparent. Top right: Believed to be No. 18 *Ningwood* departing for Cowes with the fireman collecting the tablet from the signalman. The supporting wires and guys referred to earlier are apparent.

Bottom: Newport shed in its BR heyday. Three 'O2' are visible, L to R, Nos. 35, *Freshwater*, 34 *Bembridge* and 30 *Shorwell*, also an unidentified 'E1'. Hard to imagine with so much railway activity and infrastructure all has now been swept away.

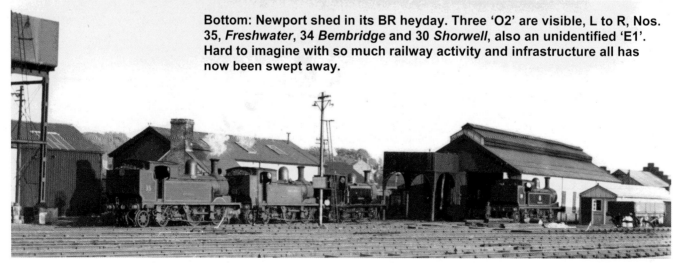

Top: No 23 *Totland* arriving from Cowes and entering the north end of the loop at Newport. The train has just passed the Up home signal, No. 2 in the frame which stood 265 yards from the signal box.

Middle: Progressing on from Newport towards Cowes was a Halt 65 feet long and siding at Cement Mills, close to which we have Antony Bennett's photograph of No. 20 *Shanklin* on a train bound for Cowes on 2 October 1965. The River Medina is widening out at this point and in the background can be seen the PS *Medway Queen* on the east side of the river. The simply constructed Halt was built in timber and was similar to that provided at Medina Wharf. The date it opened is uncertain but it was referred to in official documents in 1870 so must have been in use by then.

Bottom: An unidentified 'O2' is seen here crossing Cement Mills Viaduct with an up train on 19 February 1966. This was originally of wooden construction and crossed a river tributary and marshy land at this point. It was rebuilt in 1880, strengthening the structure significantly, the cast iron piles clearly seen here. The nearby cement mills (seen in the background here behind the viaduct) occupied a position by the river in a somewhat cramped site and were served by a siding leading off the main line facing the down direction allowing direct access for chalk trains from Shide quarry. The contract for chalk traffic was significant; at its peak some 6,000 wagon loads representing 50,000 tons annually were handled. The siding had a run round loop within the site and it also contained a small tramway system. Owing to the light flat-bottomed rail in the sidings, the 'A1X' class 0-6-0T engines were retained to serve this lucrative traffic. The works here at one time employed about 100 men.

1.

2.

3.

4.

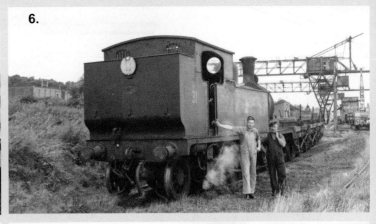

1. Between Newport and Cowes was the extensive sidings at Medina Wharf established in 1878 for unloading coal and general merchandise. It was extensively modernised by the SR in 1928 and was very much the haunt of the class 'E1' 0-6-0Ts. Here an unidentified member of the class shunts coal wagons ready to take on to Newport. It shared with St Helens the point at which a number of items of rolling stock and locomotives from the mainland were unloaded. From 1925 the use of Medina Wharf was accelerated for this purpose.

2. A general view of the sidings close to the end of a rail connection on 10 August 1966. Even at this date activity can be seen in the shape of empty coal wagons probably now being used to transport track ballast and bolster wagons for movement of rail.

3. No. 31 *Chale* shunts some rail carrying bolster wagons at the Wharf on the same date. Note the light flat bottomed track still extant in the sidings here, normally the class 'O2's would not operate here, but by this time nobody cared anymore. Until 1912 a signal box controlled access from the main line and was a staff station until abolished and replaced by a ground frame.

4. Unloading rails from a motor barge on 10 August 1966. The River Medina is tidal at this point, the barge will move off on the next high tide. When constructed the wharf enjoyed some 10 feet of water at low tide, but general silting up reduced this over the years.

5. Another general view taken on 3 September 1965 and on the left in the background one of the coal transporters. The primary traffic handled here was coal, a considerable quantity being shipped in from the County Durham pits. The original wooden Jetty was replaced by a purpose built concrete wharf with additional landing facilities by the SR in the late 1920s along with increased siding mileage, as seen here. The cost of this was just shy of £100,000 as additional unforeseen expenditure arose during the works. The old jetty was demolished in 1932.

6. Driver Prouten (on right) and his Fireman take a break from shunting and pose for the photographer at Medina Wharf with their charge No. 31 *Chale* on 10 August 1966.

7. The view from a brake van as a coal train leaves the Wharf on to the main line heading for Newport hauled by No. 27 *Merstone* on 3 September 1965. The staff member appears to be checking the wagon brakes as the heavy load trundles on her way up the incline from the quayside sidings. The Ground Frame controlling entry to Medina Wharf sidings that replaced the earlier signal box in 1912 can just be seen on the right.

8. A last look at Medina Wharf, this time a passenger train pulling away from the passenger platform provided here for those alighting or joining having business at the Wharf. It is unclear when this was opened but it was referred to in 1910. It was a basic short wooden platform which could effectively only handle one or two carriages. Needless to say it wasn't photographed extensively so images are hard to find. The Wharf is off to the right in this view; the platform also hiding behind the tree.

Left: Mill Hill was a suburb of Cowes and is seen here on 5 January 1966. The sharpness of the 10 chain radius right hand curve is very obvious and not ideal for operational purposes, although it was not thought necessary to be provided with a check rail. From sometime around 1885 a siding existed south of the station facing down trains. It didn't exist for very long as it was removed circa 1913 to allow both easement of the curve and extension to the platform. The glazed extension on the end of the station building gives the appearance of a greenhouse! The access point to the ticket office can be clearly seen.

Bottom: The station on 14 October 1961, with a train from Cowes entering the station. Note the interesting design of the valancing on the station building and canopy, no doubt a type favoured by the building contractor employed by the then Cowes & Newport Railway Company a few years prior to their amalgamation forming the Isle of Wight Central Railway Company. The gate giving access to the station is visible here just behind the couple and child getting ready to board the train. As indicated here the station was located conveniently for a large number of residential properties in the immediate area.

Right: Mill Hill station was located immediately at the southern end of the 210 yard long tunnel (some sources say 208 yards - perhaps it depended if the measurement was on the inside or the outside of the curve?) and actually only 36 chains from Cowes station. The station building dates from 1879 and was largely unaltered until closure of the line in 1966. Out of sight around the right-hand curve was once located a small signal box controlling signals but these were removed in the early years of the 20th century.

Bottom: Here the 3:33pm Ryde to Cowes train is about to leave Mill Hill for the short trip to Cowes on 24 May 1964. The engine is No. 17 *Seaview,* one of the late survivor 'O2's being withdrawn in 1967. Access from Artic Road to the station was by means of the path on the left, the gate just in view. Interestingly the base of the platform lamp is painted white for sighting, usually thought of as a feature in wartime but felt necessary here given the narrowness of the platform.

Opposite top left: Cowes arrival. The engine has drawn up to the buffers and the next stage will be to check all is clear with no more passengers left to disembark before propelling the train clear of the engine release crossover.

Opposite top right: With the coaches safely out of the way and secure, the engine runs forward again to reach the crossover. Once clear of the points and with these restored to their 'normal' position, the coaches will be gravity shunted under the control of the Guard to come to rest close to the buffers.

Opposite bottom: Arriving at Cowes with a through train from Ventnor via Merstone as indicated by the headcode is No. 14 *Fishbourne*. We may be able to date this view to 1956 as it appears the BR emblem on the side tank is the later version introduced that year, coupled to the closure of the Merstone

route also that year. The entry into the station was on an eight chain radius curve necessitated by existing buildings in the town.

This page top: No. 35 *Freshwater* entering Cowes on 25 June 1957. The original station dating from the 1862 opening of the Cowes & Newport Railway was remodelled by the IWCR in 1918 to provide extended down and up platforms (325 and 300 feet respectively) plus a new bay platform. Some sidings were also extended. The signal box was moved at the same time. The footbridge did not actually serve the platforms being instead a public bridge to allow pedestrians to move between Terminus Road and Cross Street. The van on the right occupies the 1918 bay platform. Notice too the check-rail necessitated by the sharp curve.

This page right: The re-sited Cowes signal box following the 1918 station improvements. Originally a 16 lever Saxby & Farmer design box located on the down platform, it was moved onto a new base and extended at the far end to allow a 22 lever frame to be fitted. The new layout required further ground signals hence the need to extend the frame. Note the brickwork of the base of the box does not look terribly uniform suggesting the work was somewhat hurried to be completed.

Opposite top: The interesting operating procedure at Cowes is shown here as No. 27 *Merstone* has reversed her train back to clear the crossover. The guard will have screwed down the brakes from his van. The engine then takes the release crossover, followed by the guard releasing the brakes and the carriages gently run back into the platform utilising the prevailing 1 in 108 gradient.

Opposite bottom: Having conducted the procedure outlined in the previous image, *Merstone* now crosses to the far platform and reverses back to couple up for the return working. Note the casing around the air pump, fitted to a few of the class.

This page top: Cowes as it existed from the 1918 improvements until closure. Unlike the situation at Ryde, Cowes station was located away from the waterfront and passengers from and to the ferry had to negotiate a modest uphill walk more often than not burdened with their heavy luggage. The station was built on a sloping site which led to the gradient but at least enabled the use of gravity to move carriages.

Arriving passengers on entering the station had to climb a flight of steps to reach the platforms, where a booking office, waiting rooms and a refreshment room were provided. The down side platform was longer than the up side at 325 feet as opposed to 300 feet. The short bay platform just out of sight on the right was added in 1918. In the early years the IWC company offices were located on the ground floor of the station building, but these moved to Newport probably at the time the new joint Newport station opened in 1875. For the record the locomotive here is No. 21 *Sandown* having pulled forward from the train she had brought in from Ryde and will shortly take the release crossover.

This page bottom: A rather grubby *Freshwater* awaits departure from Cowes, thought to be early in 1966. The curvature of the platform is clear here requiring passengers to '*mind the gap*'. The extension to the coal bunkers on the Island based 'O2's can be seen clearly which significantly increased coal capacity from one and a half tons to three and a quarter tons.

3 Newport to Sandown

This page top: Taken looking south after 1956 can be seen the two impressive viaducts carrying the lines from Ryde (left) and Sandown (right) into Newport station. The Sandown line has been removed by the time of the photograph but the track bed can be seen. The bracket signal has of course had the former arm signalling trains on to the Sandown line removed. In the early days before major changes to the Engine Shed and yard, a siding dropped steeply down to the Quay, crossing the Medina basin by a wooden lifting bridge with a wagon turntable enabling wagons to be loaded direct to/from barges.

This page left: Here we have an interesting view of the Sandown line viaduct pairing away to take a more southerly direction towards Shide. Taken on 8 July 1959 it shows track removal underway some three years since the route was closed to all traffic. Coppins Bridge can be seen in the background, the side girders being held by cross struts giving it the impression of a cage for the train to pass through.

Opposite top: Entering Shide on 17 August 1955 is 'E1' Class No. 2 *Yarmouth* on the 4:08pm train. *Yarmouth* was to survive just one more year after this photograph was taken, being withdrawn in September 1956. Like many rural Island stations it was located hard by a level crossing. The station building contained a booking office and waiting room, no canopy was provided. The signal box seen here was in fact a replacement probably put in during or just before 1896. Despite its close proximity on the outskirts of Newport, Shide was a block post. A long siding existed up through a tunnel into a large chalk pit on St Georges Down. This chalk traffic was worked by the remaining 'A1X' class 0-6-0Ts owing to the light track used on the siding and formed transfer trips to Cement Mills on the Cowes line.

Opposite bottom: Blackwater was a short distance from Shide and served the small community there and to an extent the village of Rookley a mile or so away by road. Here a Sandown bound train awaits departure behind No. 28 *Ashey* in January 1956, the year this line closed. Originally the platform was rather short at 173 feet but this was later extended to 246 feet in 1912. A six lever frame located in the station building operated the signals.

Top: 28 January 1956 was clearly a wet overcast day as No. 28 *Ashey* pulls away from Merstone with a train for Sandown. The roof of the original station house can be seen above the engine. The new facilities came into use on the east side of the road crossing just prior to the opening of the line to St Lawrence in 1897 (extended to Ventnor West in 1900). The remains of this line curving away to the right are already hard to define some four years after closure. The crossing gates here were the only ones on the Island to be operated by a gate wheel in the signal box, all others being hand operated. The box was supplied by Saxby & Farmer and had a 28 lever frame. The walkway from the platform slope to the road replaced a subway which regularly filled up with water so was filled in. Some wagons can just be seen on the siding originally provided when the Newport to Sandown line opened in 1875. Two further sidings were added as part of the new station development, these were respectively on both sides of the island platform behind the photographer. Coaching stock for the Ventnor West line was frequently stored on the southernmost.

Bottom; A closer view of No. 28 *Ashey* at Merstone with a Sandown bound train. The water tower appearing above the engine was fed from a water supply that ironically used to constantly flood the original subway access to the platform. The station house beyond the crossing was part of the original station but then served as staff accommodation. The station master here in 1915 according to Kellys Directory was Fred Mew.

A Sandown bound train draws into Horringford in 1955 under the watchful eye of a member of the station staff. At the head of the train is No. 16 *Ventnor*. A 180 foot platform was provided here west of the road crossing and a single siding sufficed for goods traffic. The station building was larger than that provided on other intermediate stations on this line, it had been temporarily the terminus of the line until opened through to Sandown. The station was not far from Arreton so served that village too. A small ground frame was located in the station offices.

A clean No. 30 *Shorwell* with a through Sandown to Cowes service recorded near to Horringford.

Above: A Sandown to Newport train entering Newchurch in 1955 hauled by No. 16 *Ventnor*. The station was of light construction in wood including the platform; it is likely this may have been owing to the abundant marshy land in this area and an attempt to reduce weight or simply to save money! Some elements of the buildings here may have been second hand from elsewhere on the system. The stretcher cabinet is fairly dominant in this view. The siding seen here on the left was provided in 1886. In WW2 the station was unfortunate to receive a direct hit from an enemy bomb which may explain the lack of continuity of the timber platform.

Opposite page top left: A quiet time at Alverstone during a visit by enthusiast Dick Riley's visit on 28 January 1956. The station house seen here replaced the original one around 1911 as this had been condemned as uninhabitable. Despite the improved and enlarged accommodation, there was nothing extra for waiting passengers so they had to use what was little more than a corrugated iron bus shelter on the platform. There were never that many anyway given the sparse population in the immediate area.

Opposite page top right: Alverstone looking towards Sandown in 1956. The siding on the left was added in October 1878 and a six-lever ground frame installed to control this and signals. There were several streams criss-crossing and converging around the station area and flooding was a periodic problem for the railway to deal with.

Opposite page bottom left: The second station house photographed in 1956 just days before closure. The road was a relatively minor one but the crossing gates in this and other images show evidence of replacement either through normal wear and tear or damage from road vehicles. Like many 1950s station views, the signage still depicts Southern Railway ownership. The bicycle possibly belongs to a member of the station staff, Alverstone, having crossing gates to operate, required someone on duty for the day's timetable service.

Bottom right: Quoting from the wonderful 'Oh. Mr Porter', 'The next train's gone..!' A train heads towards Sandown from Alverstone on a January day in 1956. The would-be passenger looks unconcerned; perhaps he's arrived early for the return working. Again note the stretcher cabinet provided, such items a feature of nearly every station with staff First Aid expertise encouraged by the railway. Today the line formation provides a popular cycleway and walk from Newport to Sandown with a small number of short deviations necessary following sales of station houses and parcels of land.

One of the very few named trains to operate on the Island was 'The Tourist'. Introduced by the Southern Railway in 1933 as a successor to the previous years 'East and West Through Train', 'The Tourist' started from Ventnor calling at Wroxall, Shanklin, Sandown, Newport (reversal), Yarmouth, and Freshwater. With fewer stops than its predecessor the full journey was a credible hour and 17 minutes. The service was curtailed during WW2 but resumed immediate on 8 May 1945 only to end permanently with the closure of the Freshwater line in 1953. Carriage boards were carried but there was no similar embellishment on the locomotive.

In beautifully clean 'sunshine' livery, No. 28 *Ashey* waits in the branch platform at Sandown ready to depart for Newport. Notice at the base of the side tank a patch has been added.

4 Newport to Freshwater

Top: Nine months on from nationalisation on 21 September 1948, No. (W)34 Newport backs its train north out of Newport station in order to gain access to the Freshwater line on what was a through Shanklin to Freshwater service. (A board detailing the destination and principal stops may just be made out attached to the side of the first coach.) The engine will have already run round the coaches whilst passengers were entering at the platform.

Bottom: Rounding the curve on to the FYN junction at Newport, No. 29 *Alverstone* arrives with a train from Freshwater around 1952. The awkwardness of the junction required trains to stop adjacent to Newport North signal box and set back into the bay platform with the repeat process on the return journey. This was only avoided between 1913 and 1923 when the FYN had its own station during its independent days which was located just out of sight beyond the last carriage. Prominent on the left skyline is the tall building forming the retort house for the former gas works.

Opposite top: No. 34 *Bembridge* taking the FYN line from Newport and the start of its journey west to Freshwater. This was probably the same train seen previously as the top view on page 91.

Opposite bottom: This late 1950s view from the footbridge shows the remains of some of the former FYN facilities and was always known by staff as the Freshwater Yard. The FYN station itself had long disappeared, the useful station building and signal box finding their way to be re-erected at Calbourne and Freshwater respectively. The location of the engine shed and cattle dock is marked by the remaining sidings. The solitary wagon in the centre marks the position of the former engine shed soon closed by the SR after the Grouping. The wagons in the foreground are parked on the former running line which carried on over the impressive Hunny Hill Viaduct now severed beyond the stop blocks. The large building on the left was the property of the FYN and included the Company offices. It remained in railway ownership until 1966. Not far beyond the viaduct was located Petticoat Lane crossing, the first of several on this line. Unfortunately there is a sad tale here as on 20 June 1903 the lady gatekeeper was killed after being hit by a train as she tried to save her deaf pet dog from running in front of the engine. Driver Harry Dore did all he could, but was unable to stop his engine in time.

Above: First station from Newport was Carisbrooke, seen in the background of the departing train. At this time it was quite a rural location so removed from the built up area it is today, the scene here now obliterated apart from a small hump in the college playing field to mark the station site. Going back in time to 7 September 1953 Class 'O2' No. 31 *Chale* pulls away from the station on the 2:40pm train from Newport to Freshwater, just two weeks away from closure. The station was some way from the now subsumed village of Carisbrooke and even further from the Castle, the obvious appeal for the discerning traveller, famous for the imprisonment of Charles 1 in 1647/8. The siding shows clear signs of lack of use and bereft of any weed killing activity. Following closure, it was then the policy of British Railways to leave the infrastructure of such lines intact for three years at this time in the unlikely situation that a case for reopening emerged. Of course it never did for the Freshwater line and track lifting commenced that year from the Newport end. Originally a second platform and passing loop was provided from the opening of the line but was found to be unnecessary for passing trains and the loop was out of use by 1913, despite efforts by station master Henry Priestley to generate traffic to justify it. So traffic never developed as the FYN Directors had hoped which was not helped from the fact there was no direct road access to the station. A rather unfortunate accident occurred on 22 August 1894 when passengers on the last train from Freshwater on Sunday evening had an unpleasant and rather alarming experience. All went well until nearing Carisbrooke station shortly after 8pm when instead of keeping to the main track the train went off on to the siding, crashing into five chalk-laden trucks standing there. The sound of the collision was heard a good distance around and a number of people were quickly attracted to the scene of the accident. Fortunately the train, which had slowed down to stop at the station, kept the metals and was not damaged, but the force of the impact naturally had the effect of severely shaking the passengers, among whom quite a panic prevailed for a time. The blame for not checking the setting of the points was attributed to a temporarily acting station master standing in for Mr Priestley, the regular man at Carisbrooke who was ill.

Opposite top: Watchingwell was originally a private station for the benefit of the owner of Swainston Manor Estate and his guests. Trains stopped here on request, passengers intending to join operated the appropriate signal using the ground frame. Passengers intending to alight were required to inform the Guard. The station opened in 1897 and remained unaltered throughout its life. It had been promised by the FYN Company to Sir Barrington Simeon to provide a station with facilities for him from the opening of the line but it failed to materialise other than a basic platform and it took legal threats before a small station building was erected. Evidence of remaining milk traffic can be seen in this view despite imminent closure. The Swainston estate encompassed the station and the manor house is off to the right, the churns almost certainly emanating from the estate farms. The notice announcing closure of the line can be seen in this view. The station house survives today.

Opposite bottom: Leaving Watchingwell and threading the Swainston Estate, No. 33 *Freshwater* heads west. The SR undertook a number of improvements on the line in the late 1920s including replacing the light flat bottomed track to allow the 'O2' class engines to work the route. The ubiquitous concrete fence posts replaced most of the deteriorating wooden posts of the FYN. Not all however as some are even visible today.

This page: Calbourne shortly after closure with facilities intact. This station continued to be manned until the final day of service owing to the need for operating the crossing and signals. From 1925 signals and points to the siding behind the platform were operated by two ground frames and the signal box taken out of use. Block instruments were transferred to the booking office. The station nameboard only carried the name of Calbourne although timetable references quote 'Calbourne & Shalfleet'. The station was roughly equal distance from both villages, the road linking the villages was Station Road but renamed Elm Road following closure. In the years between the wars the Station Master was William Henley who became increasingly deaf and his wife Molly was allowed to take on some duties including operating the crossing gates, thus allowing William to stay in post.

Above: No. 32 *Bonchurch* **crossing Calbourne Viaduct circa 1952. This viaduct constructed in iron was one of two on this line, the other being Hunny Hill in Newport. It was roughly 237 feet long built on steel trestles about 28 feet apart. It took the line over a river tributary called the Caul Bourne.**

Opposite top: Conventional working at Ningwood with No. 31 *Chale* **bound for Newport. In the distance a Freshwater train has just departed. The small signal box here contained just nine levers, the interlocking such that only one train could arrive at a time, this was due to the fact there was no Clearing Point (the 440yd 'overrun') ahead of either starting signal. Levers 4 and 5 worked the facing/ trailing points at either end of the loop, the facing points lock activated by the same lever that moved the respective turnout. As is described below, the box could be switched out and long-section working established at which point the distant signals would also become operational. To achieve switching out, no single line staff could be out for a train in the section either side of Ningwood, the points Nos 4 and 5 set normal for the Down platform and the home, starting and distant signal cleared. With the co-operation then of the signalman either side, the Interlocking lever (No. 9) could be reversed and after the men either side had tested long section working, Ningwood was switched out of circuit. To switch back in the reverse applied although again with the co-operation of the men either side, no train in section and the necessary test carried out to both Freshwater and Newport. Post 1928, Ningwood was the only crossing place between the two ends of the line and was chosen as such for its geographical position nearest to the mid point of the railway rather than for the traffic handled.**

Opposite bottom: No. 30 *Shorwell* **heading a Freshwater to Newport train at Ningwood. This early 1950s view shows the train using the Down platform even though it is travelling in the Up (Newport) direction and so taking advantage of the signalling changes made by the SR in 1927 allowing the signal box to be switched out at certain times when a long-section staff Newport to Freshwater was used. The up and down signals can be seen here being in the "off" position. Engines usually worked smokebox first to Freshwater so this working is rather unusual. Following closure, apart from removal of the signal arms and other reusable items, much of the infrastructure remained. The station building remained boarded up for some years but fortunately it still survives today albeit with several extensions to make it a fine private home. The water tower was added by the SR in the late 1920s. At this time as with most stations on this line there was one member of staff who as jack of all trades performed duties as Porter, Signalman, Booking Clerk and 'Station Master' although the latter role was of course never defined as such. Carisbrooke and Watchingwell were unstaffed Halts in later years, but owing to its level crossing Calbourne station remained staffed.**

Opposite top: 'O2' No. 29 *Alverstone* at Yarmouth with a four coach train on 10 September 1953. The stream running diagonally across the station site meant the second platform was offset to the main one. With the passing loop available at Ningwood it was found not to be necessary and was never signalled to pass trains. It was little used and was removed as early as 1911. A single siding (to the left of the building) was provided which faced Newport and often stabled livestock vehicles. A horsebox and cattle wagon reside, probably little or never used at this date. At one time it was proposed to extend the line to the quay but this never materialised. Back in 1911 the then station master Mr Spinks lost an arm in a shunting accident. He recovered and stayed in post for a while being replaced by Henry Hodges by 1915. George Spinks transferring to Haven Street.

Opposite bottom; Taken after closure and looking forlorn the station building was fairly modest containing the basic requirements of booking office, waiting room and toilet. The legacy of the wartime blackout regime can still be seen with white paint marking the doors and building ends. Further up the platform once existed a small signal box controlling signals and loop points, it was removed at the same time as the loop. The station building is still extant, tastefully extended in similar style and operates as a Bistro with a railway theme.

Above: This is Causeway Crossing just prior to closure of the Newport to Freshwater line in 1953. It was one of four such crossings on the branch (at Petticoat Lane, Pound Lane, Hill Place Lane, and Causeway), all provided with a small cottage for the crossing keeper. There were some variations in design and two still survive but greatly altered including the one seen here. Some are known to have had lady crossing keepers, often with their husbands in the permanent way gang. One such is here at Causeway Crossing, ably served for many years by Alice Froud in the early part of the 20th century. A bell was provided to notify Alice of any imminent train movement from the signal box at Freshwater. A footbridge was originally provided at the crossing, but found to be a luxury and was removed by the FYN and replaced instead by 'kissing gates'. Around 1906 it was found Causeway Crossing cottage needed underpinning and other improvements. It is thought the impoverished FYN Company had the cottages built on the cheap without damp courses or mains water supply.

Top: No. 33 *Bembridge* running round her train at Freshwater on 10 September 1953. The small goods yard on the right functioned until closure of the route in 1953, latterly with just delivery of coal and minerals. In the early days livestock was dealt with but as this was increasingly travelling by road, facilities including the end loading dock and some sidings were removed. The ground here was (and still is) very marshy and probably accounts for the unevenness of the platform and 'wonky' fencing and station nameboard. The FYN Company had to drain the area for their station in the 1880s so perhaps further settling over the years was not unexpected. Following the Grouping and absorption into the Southern Railway system (delayed until August 1923 by financial wranglings), a programme of improvements took place including demolition of the engine shed and carriage shed. Very little remains today, the goods shed still stands and part of the station platform, both now forming part of Honor & Jeffries Garden Centre. The FYN station master for many years was Samuel Urry who had transferred from the IWCR and was later absorbed into the SR.

Middle: No. 27 *Merstone* awaiting departure. The platform was extended on several occasions to cope with lengthened trains. The first extension in FYN days occurred in Sept 1907 and the stream diverted. The work done by William Wheeler, a local builder, for £111-6s-0d including fencing and a gate. As will be seen from the lower image, the furthest extension was undertaken by the SR after taking over the line was quite narrow, a result of a stream immediately behind it. The signal box seen in front of the station building was a replacement originating from the FYN station at Newport replacing a rather dilapidated one located at the end of the platform. The FYN signal boxes were tiny affairs and little more than garden sheds! The one seen here was soon to be removed and served as a bus shelter locally in School Green Road for many years until removal again, this time rescued by the IoW Steam Railway and placed at Wootton, a remarkable survivor.

Bottom: Ready to depart Freshwater sometime in 1949 or 1950 we have No. 32 *Bonchurch* in the early lined BR livery. The ubiquitous concrete fence panels reveal the origins of the platform extension made by the SR in 1926 anticipating the need to accommodate longer trains as day tripper numbers were increasing. Some of this increase came in consequence of the introduction of 'The Tourist' which ran daily (Sundays excepted). The FYN tried something slightly similar in 1905 offering cheap return tickets from Freshwater to Shanklin calling them 'evenings by the sea'. All a bit bizarre given Freshwater Bay was only a 15 minute walk from Freshwater station..!

5 Brading to Bembridge

Top: An early 1950s scene with an unidentified 'O2' (possibly No. 16 *Ventnor*) about to enter Brading from Ryde. The Bembridge branch is curving away to the right from the main line. The state of the track indicates that closure to regular passenger trains has already taken place suggesting this view dates from around 1954 (it continued as a siding to St Helens until 1957, used periodically for moving condemned rolling stock). The branch at this point first existed as a goods only line to Brading Quay from the early days of the Ryde to Ventnor line. The sidings at the Quay fell into disuse when the Bembridge branch opened to St Helens and facilities there assumed dominance.

Right: No. 20 *Shanklin* in the course of running round the Bembridge branch train at Brading in the early 1950s; again the replacement starting signals for the Bembridge branch may be seen. From the smoke issuing the fireman is also attending to his duties prior to setting off.

Above: No. 23 *Totland* standing in the platform at the only intermediate station on the branch, St. Helens with a Bembridge to Brading service. Much of the branch was carried across a low embankment which required many tons of chalk and clay to provide a sound base before track laying could commence. The background is dominated by the local gas works. Just visible also is the gated siding leading to the Harbour.

Opposite bottom; The 3:52pm train from Bembridge to Brading approaches St Helens station in 1952. This view shows the siding to the quay with the catch point protecting the running line. The quay was quite extensive with a transhipment goods shed, engine shed, two cranes (one being a mobile steam crane), a weighbridge, and several sidings varying in length from 440 to 600 feet and also a wagon turntable. Coal and minerals were the most common traffic handled but it also received rolling stock from the mainland, sharing this role with Medina Wharf. The latter gradually assumed dominance after its reconstruction in the late 1920s and the importance of St Helens reduced accordingly. A little known short-lived train ferry operated from St Helens Quay to Langstone on the Hayling Island branch from 1885 to 1888 carrying coals and goods wagons from the mainland. Unfortunately the venture was not successful as the ferry found it difficult to negotiate open seas in rough weather and it failed to make a profit.

Above: St Helens facing Bembridge after the 1953 closure. The track is still in situ but now disrupted by the installation of a pipeline in progress. The station changed very little over the years and is much the same in this view as it would have been as constructed in 1877. The gasometer clearly marking the location of the gas works. Siding access was provided from the north quay siding complex. This spurred off just beyond the station as the main line curved away to the right.

Right: Taken close to Bembridge station after closure in 1953, this shows the branch curving away towards St Helens. An old wagon body provided a shelter and lock-up for the permanent way gang. The harbour is off to the right. The line from Brading to St Helens was opened for goods traffic in August 1878, but delays owing to the need to build up the formation and embankment between St Helens and Bembridge prevented full opening until May 1882.

No. 14 *Fishbourne* at the Bembridge terminus and soon ready to return to Brading: although the engine crew are taking the opportunity for a break in the sunshine for the present! The substantial station building made a statement by the little Bembridge Harbour Improvement Railway Company (BHIR) which opened to goods traffic in 1879 but not until 1882 for passenger traffic. It was worked by the IWR until the IWR took over ownership in 1898. Bembridge Harbour never developed in the way it was envisaged and the line never made a profit and inevitably became an early Island railway closure. As at Ventnor, to save space a sector plate was provided to gain access to the run round loop. Often referred to as a turntable this was not strictly the case as it was not designed to turn locomotives through 180 degrees. As was typical of so many locations both on the Island and elsewhere, a spare passenger coach waits in the siding should demand dictate it be necessary to strengthen the branch service.

6 Merstone to Ventnor West

Above: The presence of the tail lamp above the right hand buffer indicates this is pull-push working arrived at Merstone from Ventnor West early in the British Railways era. The engine is 'A1X' No. 13 *Carisbrooke* in smart livery. Trains to and from Ventnor West could only access this platform which was officially known as 'No. 2 road'.

Left: A tall and rather studious looking crew member on No. 13 seen in close up, his size confirming the diminutive size of the actual engine he is on. The decorative valance to the canopy at Merstone is indication of how aesthetics were so important to the Victorian railway builders.

Above: Here we have three more in the sequence of images featuring No. 13 *Carisbrooke,* one of the last class 'A1X's to return to the mainland. Although Ventnor West trains could only use this side of the island platform, services to and from Sandown could use either. Note the striped paint pattern on the station name board and lamp, a legacy of WW2 and the blackout conditions. The number 22 on the smokebox is again the crew roster number.

Opposite top: No. 13 *Carisbrooke* sweeps around the curve towards the junction at Merstone with the 9.25am service. According to the photographer this was a service from Merstone but it will be noted the tail lamp is still in position on the front of the locomotive. Likely the crew who would spend all day shuttling to and fro simply did not bother with changing such peripherals. Services on the branch were rarely more than two carriages but were supplemented in busier summer months if needed. When several of the 'A1X' type were returned to the mainland in 1949 (including *Carisbrooke*), the 'O2's became more of the regular engines to work services on the line. The bracket signal controlling entry for trains on the Sandown line (Nos. 23 and 26 in the frame) can be seen in the background with both platforms at Merstone signalled for bi-directional working so far as trains between Newport and Sandown were concerned.

Opposite bottom: No. 13 again with the 2.00pm Ventnor West to Merstone, possibly close to the previous location although this time the aforementioned signal is not visible although perhaps still on the same day. For the final years of its life, the branch was worked using a single train-staff which was used to unlock the intermediate ground frames.

Unfortunately images of two of the intermediate stations on the Ventnor West line, namely Godshill and St Lawrence have proven impossible to locate within the archive. As has been the case elsewhere in the UK often the last lines to open have been the first to close, the line to Ventnor West closing in 1952. A few notes of interest will hopefully make for some of the shortfall.

At Godshill the station was located at the extreme west end of the village but reasonably walkable for the fit and healthy. The line was fairly straight on the approaches to the single platform which was some 300 feet in length. The station building incorporated the station master's house with a single storey addition housing the usual booking office, waiting room, staff room and toilets. A single siding existed of some 180 feet with entry facing the Merstone direction. Godshill became an unstaffed Halt probably c1926 along with St Lawrence. The station building which was also very similar to that at neighbouring Whitwell is still extant today as a private dwelling.

At St Lawrence the station was located somewhat precariously along a shelf in the rock which stretched out along the Undercliff from Niton to Ventnor. Facilities were squeezed into this space resulting in a narrow single platform and a station house facing out onto Seven Sisters Road. A short siding was provided on the other side of the road bridge. The station was a temporary terminus from 1897 until 1900 and acted as the station for Ventnor, during this time called 'Ventnor (St Lawrence)'. A temporary run-round loop was provided at the eastern extremity just beyond the goods siding, evidence of which soon disappeared when the extension to Ventnor Town opened after three years of use. The first station master here was thought to be Mr E. Wadmore who left in 1912. Falls from the steep cliff face were fairly common, the most significant occurred in 1903. Not just rocks however, there are reports of sheep tumbling down on to the line from grazing too close to the edge!

Above: 'O2' No. 27 *Merstone* at Whitwell with the 1.25pm Merstone to Ventnor West service. (It is pure coincidence that a number of the photographs used in this book show an engine with the same name as the location.) Evidence of greater times is apparent with the former passing loop and second platform out of use together with the signal box since 1932. The signal box which had stood at the Merstone end of the former down platform had 10 working levers. Out of sight behind the engine and the station buildings there was a small goods yard and also a dock siding. Following the rationalisation this was accessed from a two lever ground frame unlocked by an Annett's key on the train staff although traffic was probably very limited. It is known some of the Waterloo 'top-brass', possibly the SR directors paid a visit to the line in the 1920s and realistically can hardly have been impressed with the level of traffic on the branch.

Top: Owing to the light permanent way the 'A1X's were ideal for the branch until relaying by the SR took place and the class 'O2's started to appear. Here 'A1X' No. 13 *Carisbrooke* waits with a Ventnor West service either late in 1948 or early in 1949. Being fitted for push-pull working she was a regular engine on the line through the 1930s and 1940s. Renumbered from No. 3 in 1932, *Carisbrooke* was returned to the mainland in May 1949 which helps to date the photograph. Thankfully Whitwell station survives today as a marvellously sympathetic restoration to its former glory and serves as a B&B establishment. The line from Merstone to St Lawrence opened in 1897, the last addition to the Island rail network. The extension into Ventnor followed in 1900.

As well as removal of the passing loop and signal box, later economies on the branch included the booking office at Whitwell only opening for the summer timetable period.

Right: No. 13 again, seen leaving for Ventnor. One passenger at least - leaning from the carriage window - was present whilst it may be noted this time the crew have covered both eventualities with the correct head code disc and also a tail lamp! The grass covered platform says it all.

Above: In open countryside near to Whitwell, 'O2' No. 36 *Carisbrooke* works the 1.25 Merstone to Ventnor West. This engine (formerly SR No. 198) was a late arrival to the Island in 1949 and took the name from the 'A1X' No. 13 upon that engine's return to the mainland in the same year. With both a head code disc and a tail lamp we still have no idea whether the train is pulling or pushing! An average journey time of 20 minutes applied for the journey of 6¾ miles between Merstone and Ventnor West. Whitwell was the location of the only level crossing on the Ventnor West line.

Opposite page: An excellent shot of the terminus at Ventnor West showing the facilities in their final years; little changed in fact since the opening in 1900. The Newport, Godshill & St Lawrence company (NGSLR) had great expectations of their line, anticipating taking traffic away from the IWR station and suitably called their station Ventnor Town to reflect the fact it was on more of a level with it and not "*half way up a mountain*". It still only got as far as Ventnor Park, built on land purchased from the Steephill Castle estate. It could have penetrated further into Ventnor past the Royal Hotel to The Grove (now a car park); some NGSLR Directors were indeed keen but the money ran out. Despite the stunning sea views for passengers as they burst out of High Hat Tunnel and along the ledge past St Lawrence, the traffic levels never materialised with passengers preferring to travel from Ryde to the IWR station. The second platform proved to be completely unnecessary from an operational perspective and soon fell into disuse. By the 1920s further economies brought about push-pull working and one-engine-in-steam, allowing stations to be unmanned. Ventnor Town was renamed Ventnor West by the SR soon after they took over in 1923. The substantial station building has survived and been converted into two separate accommodation units. A blue plaque now denotes its origins. The station area and approaches have been developed into a small housing estate.

Left: Happy in their work, Driver Frank Ash (left) and Fireman Terry Hatcher. Courtesy Jane Moat.

Right: Emerging through the shrubbery, a train having just passed the Quarry siding enters Ventnor West station behind No. 36 *Carisbrooke* sometime in late 1949 of early 1950. The signal post is of interest as the three arms denote entry (top to bottom) Platform 1, Platform 2 and oddly the third being entry to the goods yard on the left which was the opposite of normal practice which would be top to bottom, signalling lines left to right; all adding to the quirkiness of this line.

Above: No. 27 *Merstone*, in the first British Railways light green livery, in the process of running back on to her train around 1949. *Merstone* also worked services on the last day of the branch on 13 September 1952. Although push-pull working was the most common mode, conventional working still featured if an engine fitted for the purpose was not available. The signal box is switched out as denoted by the appropriate entry and exit signals being 'off', the line effectively being operated as one engine in steam with a key on the train staff used to unlock the points to facilitate running round. The original starting signal supplied by Railway Signal Company was soon to be replaced by an upper quadrant SR rail built version as seen on the previous page. A spare carriage can be seen beyond the yard crane.